# WHAT IS A
# DICTATORSHIP?

## NICK HUNTER

raintree
a Capstone company — publishers for children

Raintree is an imprint of Capstone Global Library Limited, a company incorporated in England and Wales having its registered office at 264 Banbury Road, Oxford OX2 7DY – Registered company number: 6695582

www.raintree.co.uk
myorders@raintree.co.uk

Produced for Raintree by Calcium
Edited by Sarah Eason and John Andrews
Designed by Keith Williams
Picture research by Rachel Blount
Production by Victoria Fitzgerald
Originated by Capstone Global Library Ltd © 2017
Printed and bound in Hong Kong

ISBN 978 1 4747 3111 9
20 19 18 17 16
10 9 8 7 6 5 4 3 2 1

**British Library Cataloguing in Publication Data**
A full catalogue record for this book is available from the British Library

**Acknowledgements**
We would like to thank the following for permission to reproduce photographs: Dreamstime: Americanspirit 35, Tom Craig 38, Thomas Dutour 39, Edwardje 32, Jose Manuel Espigares Garcia 31, Juergen2008 37, Kelvintt 36, Georgios Kollidas 18, Konradbak 29, Dejan Ljami 30, Linqong 43, Lucian Milasan 24, Natursports 40, Pressureua 25, Simonwedege 16, Vasily Smirnov 41, Raluca Tudor 19, Victoo 33; German Federal Archive: 5, 13; Shutterstock: Solodov Alexey 11, Asianet-Pakistan 34, Atomazul 27, Brandonht 42, Hung Chung Chih 14, Fernando Cortes 1, 9, Duckeesue 22, Featureflash 7, Oleg Golovnev 12, Joe Gough 44, Andrey Grinyov 8, Sadik Gulec 4, Douglas Knight 20, Georgios Kollidas 10, Giancarlo Liguori 45, Arkady Mazor 6, RM 21, Scruggelgreen 17, Maxim Tupikov 23, Jiri Vaclavek 26, Ahmad Faizal Yahya 28; Wikipedia Commons: Jjron 15.

Cover art reproduced with permission of: Wikipedia Commons: Jjron (left); Shutterstock: Frontpage (right).

# Contents

# CHAPTER ONE

# What is a dictatorship?

In many countries around the world, the president or prime minister is chosen by the people in an election. All adult **citizens** have a vote and can vote for someone else at the next election if they dislike the way their country is being governed. Millions of people who live in countries ruled by **dictatorship** have no choice about who leads their country.

## UNDERSTANDING DICTATORSHIPS

A dictatorship is a form of government in which one person or a small group of people hold total power. There is no elected body that limits their power and the people they govern cannot vote for a different government at elections. Dictatorships usually seize power by force, particularly in times of national turmoil or emergency, such as during a war.

*Many innocent people in Syria have been injured or killed during protests against the dictatorship of the country's president, Bashar al-Assad.*

## PERSONAL OR PARTY DICTATORSHIP

Sometimes a dictator is a single person, but often **absolute power** is held by a group such as a **political party** that has banned all elections or other political groups. A dictatorship may also be a combination of the two. Adolf Hitler was dictator of Germany between 1933 and 1945 but was also leader of the Nazi Party, which formed the country's government.

Adolf Hitler was in complete control of both the Nazi Party and Germany during his dictatorship.

## UNDERSTANDING BETTER

### RESTORING ORDER

Benito Mussolini was dictator of Italy between 1925 and 1943. He came to power at a time when his country was in turmoil. Mussolini promised to restore order and make Italy great again. What qualities do you think Mussolini had that might have appealed to ordinary Italians? If Mussolini achieved his goals, was his dictatorship a good thing for Italians?

# The history of dictatorships

Dictatorship has a long history. Strong, ambitious men, and sometimes women, have always wanted to hold power over others. The first dictatorships, and the first use of the word "dictator", can be found in the ancient world. However, most governments by dictators have been set up in the past 100 years. Why did it take so long for dictatorship to become established?

Joseph Stalin was dictator of the **Soviet Union**, a vast country including modern Russia, during the 1930s and 1940s. During this time, many European countries, including Germany and Italy, were ruled by dictators.

## DEMOCRACY AND THE RIGHT TO RULE

The first government elected by its people ruled the small city state of Athens in ancient Greece. A form of government in which people have a say in how their country is controlled is known as **democracy**. Although democracy was established early in Greece's history, it did not spread quickly to the rest of the world. For more than 2,000 years after the birth of democracy in Athens, most rulers around the world were not elected. However, that does not mean that dictators ruled most countries. Many countries were instead ruled by **monarchs**.

Although kings and queens once often held total power in a country or territory, they were not usually dictators. Rather than seizing power, most monarchs rose to power by being the child of the previous king or, in some cases, by **deposing** the previous king. In the Christian countries of Europe and elsewhere, people believed that monarchs were chosen by God, so they were not seen as dictators.

Unlike some other monarchs or dictators, the British Royal Family does not hold total power. They are expected to follow laws passed in the elected United Kingdom Parliament.

## UNDERSTANDING BETTER

### MONARCHY VERSUS DICTATORSHIP

Think about the differences between monarchs and dictators. Both types of ruler are not elected by their people. What else do they have in common? How are they different? Look for examples of monarchs around the world today. Why do you think they are still in power?

## THE RETURN OF DICTATORS

From the 19th century, the way in which countries were controlled began to rapidly change. Suddenly, people wanted a say in their own government. Many countries were **colonies** of foreign powers and wanted to rule themselves. As a result, monarchs were overthrown or agreed to work with an elected government. However, if this change of government was marked by unrest and fighting, it was easier for dictators to seize power. During the huge political and social changes of the 19th century, in which revolutions took place and monarchs were overthrown, dictatorships became more common.

# Dictators in the ancient world

The word "dictator" comes from ancient Rome. The first dictators were very different from our modern-day image of a dictator. Roman dictators were appointed by the Roman senate to lead the city's government during times of crisis. Normally, Roman dictators were allowed to rule only for six months or until the crisis had passed.

## GREEK TYRANTS

Our word "dictator" may have come from ancient Rome, but it is the **tyrants** who ruled some ancient Greek states who were more like the modern dictators we know today. Like Roman dictators, tyrants such as Dionysius I of Syracuse seized power during wars and invasions. The ancient Greeks believed a tyrant was anyone who seized power against the laws of the Greek democratic **constitution**. Since ancient times the word "tyrant" has come to mean any cruel and merciless ruler.

Athens in ancient Greece is known as the birthplace of democracy. However, even the democratic city state of Athens was sometimes ruled by tyrants, including, in the 6th century BC, by Pisistratus and his sons Hippias and Hipparchus.

# UNDERSTANDING BETTER

## IS IT ACCEPTABLE TO BREAK THE LAW?

"If you must break the law, do it to seize power: in all other cases observe it."

These words are from Julius Caesar, but they could apply to many dictators. Caesar himself broke the Roman law when he crossed the Rubicon River in Italy and marched his armies towards Rome in 49 BC. Why did Caesar think it was acceptable to break the law to seize power? Are his words a justification of his actions? Maybe Caesar believed that by breaking the law he would make Rome a better place? What do you think?

▲ Before he became dictator, Julius Caesar made his name across the Roman Empire as a successful military campaigner.

# The first modern dictatorships

Caesar Augustus became the first Roman **emperor** in 27 BC. He claimed absolute power and set the tone for what was to follow in the Roman Empire – and across the world – for hundreds of years thereafter. Following Augustus's reign, most countries were ruled by monarchs and emperors who passed on power to their children. If an argument took place about the next ruler, a **civil war** usually broke out and the winner would then maintain or seize power. Whichever king or queen was in charge, their rule was absolute.

### ALL CHANGE

Monarchy power systems began to change in the late 18th century. Britain's colonies in North America declared themselves independent in 1776. These United States declared that they would be ruled by an elected president and **congress**. In 1789, the people of France overthrew King Louis XVI in a chaotic and bloody revolution that plunged much of Europe into war.

### THE RISE OF NAPOLEON

Napoleon Bonaparte made himself **consul** and then emperor of France in 1804, to bring order to the country. Napoleon was able to do this because of his military successes across Europe.

Napoleon's dictatorship ended when he was defeated on the battlefield. He is still widely seen as one of the greatest figures in French history.

CCCP

ВСЯ ВЛАСТЬ СОВЕТАМ!

30 коп

ЕНИНА почта 1960

▲ *Lenin and the Bolsheviks claimed to rule Russia in the name of the people, but to many onlookers they seemed to be just another form of dictatorship.*

Napoleon's many achievements included setting up a legal system that is still used in France today. Although Napoleon held total power and used a network of spies to maintain control over France, his rule shows that dictators are not always bad for their people.

## NEW DICTATORSHIPS

After Napoleon, dictators took power in many South American countries that had been ruled before by Spain. Dictators appeared in states in which there was no other government. In 1917, the Russian emperor was overthrown in a revolution, leading to a period of uncertain rule in Russia. Eventually, the Bolshevik Party, led by Vladimir Lenin, took over. This was a new form of dictatorship led by a political group rather than one person.

## UNDERSTANDING BETTER

### CAN DICTATORSHIP BE BENEFICIAL?

Why do you think dictatorships have often taken place in countries that were on the verge of becoming democracies? Democracy is usually seen as a better system under which to live than dictatorship, but can you think of times when this might not be true? For example, does a democracy work well in a situation in which many, sometimes violent, groups are competing for control?

# Hitler and Stalin

In the years after World War I (1914–1918), many of the world's most powerful countries were ruled by dictators. World War I was one of the most destructive conflicts in history and caused governments across Europe to fall. Economic problems led many people to feel angry with the leaders who had taken them into the war. These disgruntled people were prepared to believe the promises of dictators.

In the 1930s, newspapers, such as this one with a photograph of Stalin, were one of the main ways of communicating with people.

## POWERFUL DICTATORS

The two most powerful dictators to seize power after World War I were Adolf Hitler and Joseph Stalin. Each man was responsible for the deaths of many millions of people. Hitler **persecuted** millions of Jews and caused the deaths of millions more people by leading Germany into World War II. Joseph Stalin murdered millions of people who, he believed, opposed him.

Hitler and Stalin were both supported by strong party organizations. Hitler's National Socialist German Workers' Party, also known as the Nazi Party, gained support from the German people when their country faced economic collapse in 1933. The party was democratically elected at first but then passed laws that meant its power could not be opposed.

## WORLD WAR II

Stalin took over the Bolshevik government established by Lenin in 1924 and set about killing or **exiling** anyone who could challenge his power. He killed or exiled millions of people. However, Stalin also managed to make the Soviet Union strong enough to withstand Hitler's armies when the German dictator invaded the country during World War II. This was the most horrific war in history and claimed the lives of both Hitler and Italian dictator Mussolini, along with the lives of tens of millions of ordinary people.

## UNDERSTANDING BETTER

### CONTROLLING THE MEDIA

Hitler was one of the first dictators to realize the importance of controlling new **media** such as radio and films, and he used it to communicate his ideas. Look at this picture of one of Hitler's mass rallies. What do you think these great shows of strength were used for? How would people react when they saw film of these events?

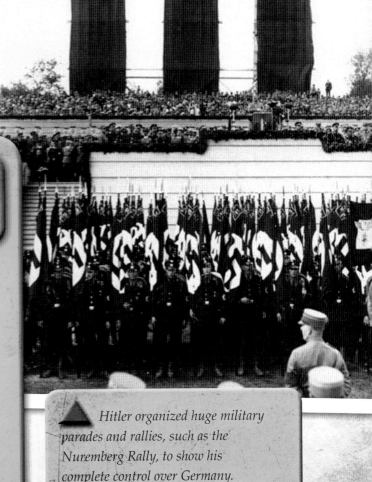

Hitler organized huge military parades and rallies, such as the Nuremberg Rally, to show his complete control over Germany.

# The Cold War

The idea of dictatorship did not die with Hitler in 1945 – Stalin remained the leader of the Soviet Union until 1953. The horror of World War II was followed by a period during which the United States and its **allies** confronted the **communist** countries led by the Soviet Union. It was also a time in which many new, independent countries broke free from the control of old empires, such as the empires of the United Kingdom and France. Conflict and political change created opportunities for many new dictators.

## MONEY AND MILITARY MIGHT

During the Cold War, Stalin and his successors in the Soviet Union provided military support and money to communist dictatorships in many parts of the world, particularly Eastern Europe. Even the democratic countries of the West were sometimes prepared to support dictators if they believed that it would mean these dictators would then turn away from the Soviet Union, and so help to stop the spread of communism across the world.

In 1949, communist forces took control of China, the world's most populous country. China's communist dictatorship is still in power today.

Saddam Hussein was put on trial and executed by the Iraqi people in 2006, after he was forced from power by a US-led invasion.

## TWENTY-FIRST CENTURY DICTATORS

Many communist dictatorships in Eastern Europe and worldwide collapsed when the Soviet Union dissolved in 1989. Without the financial and military support once provided by the Soviet Union, the dictatorships that depended upon that support fell apart. However, there are still many countries around the world that are ruled by single dictators or groups of people who cannot be voted out of power.

# UNDERSTANDING BETTER

## DICTATORSHIP STRATEGIES

Saddam Hussein was dictator of Iraq from 1979 until 2003. His rule shows some of the ways in which dictators try to keep power:

- Saddam spent much of Iraq's oil wealth on building a large, armed force and fighting a series of wars against neighbouring Iran and Kuwait. Anyone who opposed his **regime** was seen as an enemy of Iraq.

- Saddam had a network of **secret police** and **informants**, and brutally **suppressed** any opposition by any means – including the use of chemical weapons on his own people.

- The dictator used the media to convince Iraqis that he was a heroic man and the only person who could lead them.

# CHAPTER TWO

# How dictatorships work

Dictatorships are not all the same, but they usually share some common features, which are explored in this chapter. Some dictators genuinely believe that they can provide good government for their people, and sometimes their people agree. In many cases, however, dictators are more interested in gaining power and riches for themselves, their friends and their families.

## GAINING POWER

Dictatorships are usually focused on how to seize power and how to keep it. Dictators often gain power during a time of conflict and turmoil. To do so they need the support of the nation's army, or a military force large enough to stop the army overthrowing the dictator. Dictators often begin their careers as military leaders and use the military might they have built up over time to seize control of a country when the time and circumstances allow it.

*Robert Mugabe has led the African country of Zimbabwe since the 1980s. Although there are elections in the country, Mugabe's supporters have often been accused of violence and **rigging** any elections held in Zimbabwe in order to remain in power.*

## NO RULES

Dictators believe that the laws that apply to governments and most people in power do not apply to them. They will often use tricks and lies to gain power, persuading people that they have only the country's best interests at heart and that they will bring about change that will improve the lives of ordinary people. Once dictators have been voted in or have gained the support of a country's people, they change laws to suit their own needs. Remember that dictators often seize power at a time of trouble or turbulence in a country, when it is easier to take control. Once in power, dictators may then hold elections, but they are meaningless because voters are often offered only one candidate to vote for – the dictator.

# UNDERSTANDING BETTER

## DICTATOR OR LIBERATOR?

Most dictators would not use the word "dictator" to describe who they are. Often, dictators may have taken power with the promise that they will protect a country from an external threat or an inadequate government. Dictators may use a title such as the "Great Liberator" or "Father of the Revolution" to persuade people that they have seized control to improve their lives. Why do you think these leaders avoid using the word "dictator"?

*Francisco Franco was dictator of Spain from 1939 to 1975. He took over after a brutal civil war but prepared his country to become a monarchy after his death.*

# Restoring order

From ancient Rome to the modern Middle East, dictators often come to power promising to restore order. Sometimes, this may be a dictator's real reason for seizing power. At other times, the dictator may try to convince people of a crisis that does not really exist in order to take control of a country. If the people of a country can be persuaded that they are under threat or that their way of life is threatened, it is far easier to persuade them to allow a new ruler to quickly seize control with the promise of stabilizing the crisis.

## KEEPING THE PEACE?

Sometimes dictatorship may be the only way to restore order in a country. This is particularly true in a country in which many armed groups are battling for power and endangering the lives of ordinary people. To achieve peace, the dictator must have the support of a military force. Any rebellious force or group that threatens the dictator's absolute control can then be crushed. The dictator may already be in charge of the army. If not, the dictator will ensure that the military leadership is fiercely loyal to no one else.

*Ayatollah Khomeini took power in Iran after a revolution in 1979. This religious dictator promised to restore respect for an extreme form of Islam in Iran.*

If people are preoccupied, they are less likely to question what is happening around them. By deflecting a nation's attention towards a "crisis" or imminent threat, the dictator can keep an iron grip on a country and its people.

Roman dictators relied upon the might of the powerful Roman army to help them restore order.

## KEEPING POWER

In Roman times, a dictator's rule would last only long enough to restore order, but modern dictators are not normally ready to give up power so easily. To keep hold of it, they will often try to convince people that the peace and order of their country is continually under threat and that the only way to maintain stability is to keep the dictator in power.

# UNDERSTANDING BETTER

## EXTERNAL THREATS

Countries are usually at their most united when they are fighting an enemy from outside. Dictators often start conflicts with other nations for this very reason. We have already seen that Saddam Hussein took Iraq to war against neighbouring countries to strengthen his hold on power. Can you find other examples of dictators around the world who are trying to unite their people by attacking other countries or groups?

# Keeping power

**Seizing power is the immediate challenge for a dictator. However, once power has been gained, how do dictators keep hold of it? All dictatorships are different, but there are some common methods that most dictatorships rely upon in order to maintain power and control.**

## A SUPPORT TEAM

Dictators rarely hold on to power entirely by themselves. All dictators need a group of supporters to help keep them in power. We have already seen that the loyalty of armed forces is important, but dictators usually have a wider group of supporters. Adolf Hitler in Germany was supported by thousands of members of the Nazi Party who helped to make his extreme ideas seem reasonable to ordinary people. The supporters also identified and terrorized anyone who opposed Hitler.

## POWER AND PRIVILEGE

In return for their support, a dictator's helpers are given jobs in government and special privileges, such as private houses, wealth and the promise of future promotion and power. This helps to ensure the loyalty of supporters – as long as the dictator remains in power and as long as no one promises them a better deal elsewhere.

*Many dictators have used money gained from selling their country's oil to finance their regimes.*

Street art images, such as this one of Gaddafi and his son, often convey the true feelings of a country towards its dictator – feelings that are too dangerous to air in any other way.

## FAKING DEMOCRACY

Dictators will often create government **institutions** to give the impression that the country's people have a say in their government. Muammar Gaddafi ruled Libya, in North Africa, from 1969 to 2011. Although Libya's people were able to vote for representatives in the country's parliament, in reality Gaddafi retained complete power and control over the country.

# UNDERSTANDING BETTER

## POLITICS THROUGH PICTURES

In 2011, Muammar Gaddafi was finally overthrown by the Libyan people. This graffiti from the time shows Gaddafi with one of his sons, who also held a powerful position in Libya. What do you think the artist who created this picture wanted to show? How do you think that person felt when the graffiti was painted?

# Crushing rebellion

In democratic countries, people are free to say what they like about the government. As long as they stay within the law of the country, people are usually allowed to speak, write or broadcast freely. In a dictatorship, those who disagree with the government are restricted in what they can say. In many cases, people can be imprisoned or even killed for criticizing a dictator.

## PROTECTION OF THE LAW

In most democratic countries, law courts protect people from attack or imprisonment by an unjust government. Why does this not happen as well in a dictatorship? Dictators have usually broken the law by seizing power. They do not recognize sources of power other than themselves – and this includes the law. If dictators allow people to openly discuss and disagree with their policies, those people might decide to put in place an alternative government and end their dictatorship. It is vital that a dictator retains absolute control over the opinions people voice.

*In democratic countries, people have the right to protest peacefully about issues they disagree with.*

> In the secretive country of North Korea, it is believed that hundreds of thousands of men, women and children are held in prison camps because they have opposed the country's dictatorship.

## SPIES AND SECRET POLICE

In a dictatorship, the government uses many techniques to discover what people are saying and doing, and to control their words and actions. Dictatorship governments are supported by secret police and security organizations that spy on ordinary people. If someone is **suspected** of being an opponent of the government, action is swift. Suspects may face trial, but there will be little opportunity to defend themselves. Often, a suspect will simply disappear, never to be heard of again. With no independent law courts to oppose them, dictators are completely free to act as they choose.

## UNDERSTANDING BETTER

### WHAT ARE HUMAN RIGHTS?

The Universal Declaration of **Human Rights** was adopted by the **United Nations** in 1948. It includes the following words:

"Everyone has the right to freedom of opinion and expression; this right includes freedom to hold opinions without interference…"

Do you think that you have this right in your country? Can you think of countries and people who do not have these rights?

# Media and propaganda

One way in which dictators can silence their critics is by controlling media such as television, newspapers and the internet. Dictators can stop the media from carrying a range of news so that a country's citizens hear only the government's viewpoint. The government can also use media to tell people about its successes, or to even tell lies. This is **propaganda**.

### HITLER AND PROPAGANDA

Adolf Hitler understood the power of propaganda when he became the dictator of Nazi Germany. One of his closest advisers was Minister of Public Enlightenment and Propaganda Joseph Goebbels. Goebbels made films that glorified Hitler and attacked groups such as the Jews, who the Nazis presented as enemies of Germany. Propaganda helped to convince many Germans that Hitler's hatred of the Jews was justified. Hitler used propaganda to whip up a wave of hatred against German Jews, who he blamed for the country's economic downfall after World War I. The German Jews were used as a scapegoat for the country's problems, and this allowed Hitler to deflect public attention away from his vice-like grip on Germany.

In countries that have a free press, newspapers and broadcasters provide different political viewpoints. In a dictatorship, only one view is allowed – the dictator's.

# UNDERSTANDING BETTER

## THE THREAT OF ONLINE MEDIA

In the past, dictators could control everything that was printed or broadcast in a country. The global rise of the internet since the 1990s has made this very difficult. As a result, dictatorships have blocked certain sites or tried to prevent people from communicating online altogether. Why are dictators so afraid of internet communication and the effect it could have on their regimes? Consider how easy it is to post photos or other material to social networking sites such as Facebook. False online identities can make critics of dictatorship more difficult to track. What threats does the medium of social networking pose to dictatorships?

### PROPAGANDA TODAY

Dictators today still try to control the media and produce propaganda. Propaganda can include everything from giant posters of the leader on city streets to websites and other online sources that promote government viewpoints. Dictators control the news that appears on television and in other media, so that people never find out what is really happening in their country.

*Websites and other digital media are not normally limited to one country and are, therefore, much more difficult for dictators to control.*

# NEWS

### Economic Growth Picks Up

This year, all over Europe and Central Asia, emerging economies are expected to grow. It was noted that some countries in the region could be seriously affected by rising food and energy prices. Major oil exporters, which account for 15 percent of the entire world's oil, are benefiting from price increase and it contributes to economic growth and stability of the budget balance.

However, rising prices for food and fuel prices creates an additional source of vulnerability for many importing countries, noted at a press conference. In response, governments in the region proposed to increase the coverage and targeting of social protection systems to support the poor. Recommend avoiding some of the measures that were taken in the region in response to previous price increases for energy and food - such as price controls and restrictions on foreign trade and export of food. pecialists drew attention to a new problem - the growth in commodity prices, which turned out to be more significant than expected. The growth in food prices is even more serious problem in emerging markets, where central banks do not enjoy a special trust. Therefore, in these countries, they should be more careful. It is possible that for some time, the level of inflation will be somewhat higher than expected. However, according to our forecasts, we do not think that it will have a severe negative impact on economic growth. High prices for raw materials may pose a real threat to the developing countries,

### Real estate market review

This year as a whole is expected to steady but slight growth. This means that in most real estate markets will dominate the cautious mood. According to experts, renters are unlikely to seek significant investment, and actively expand in the face of uncertainty. So, they want to see evidence of the resumption of sustained growth around the world before the deal with the extension. So that the base rental rates in most major business centers in the following year will remain at about the same level as that in the past. According to the forecast, this year is possible and a marked increase in base rental rates in some cities, applying the appropriate expectations. With regard to the effect that economic growth will have on demand for space by renters in the near future, experts believe that the decisions taken by companies lease refer to the long term. In addition, the experts reviewed the changes that have occurred in the property market over the past year.

### Oil prices hit two-year high

The other day trades in oil contracts reached a 2-year high not seen since September 2008, and amounted to $ 108 per barrel. At the stock exchange price of crude oil decisively crossed the $ 120 per barrel, and the trades have not only held within close to the 2-year high, but often exceeding the record level. At present, European refineries are in a difficult position due to lack of supplied raw materials, which became one of the reasons for the increase in prices for their products. As evidenced by past expe-

# Cult of personality

One of the most common uses of propaganda in a dictatorship is to promote the leader's "cult of personality". This is a projected personality that the dictator has created through clever use of media. Dictators want people to believe they are caring, wise and strong figures. Sometimes dictators are even presented as god-like. Kings and queens first developed the cult of personality. By also presenting themselves as monarchs, dictators try to show people that, like kings and queens, they also have the right to absolute rule.

## SAPARMURAT NIYAZOV

One of the most extreme cults of personality in recent history was Saparmurat Niyazov, the dictator of Turkmenistan in central Asia. The dictator commissioned a giant revolving statue of himself, which always faced the Sun. Cities, a theme park and even a month of the year were renamed to honour the dictator. Saparmurat Niyazov also wrote a book about Turkmenistan, which was sent to every school in the country to be used as part of the curriculum. The book presented the history of the country as the dictator chose to portray it, with little regard for any historical accuracy.

In a dictatorship, the dictator's image appears everywhere. In Nazi Germany, Hitler's face even appeared on the stamps people used to send letters to each other.

## HIDING THE REAL SITUATION

Sometimes a cult of personality is created to focus attention on a single dictator, when, in reality, a group of dictators control a country. In these instances, when a political party or group seizes control of a country, they may build a cult of personality around a single figure. The world's attention is focused on the created personality, while the real power in a country lies elsewhere, such as in the leadership of the armed forces.

The cult of personality can sometimes backfire. In this demonstration, opponents of Syria's dictator Bashar al-Assad compare the leader to Hitler.

## UNDERSTANDING BETTER

### IN THE SPOTLIGHT

Why do dictators spend so much time and money creating a cult of personality? Can you see similarities between this and the way that film and music stars present themselves to the media? Celebrities try to stay in the public eye so they can continue their successful careers. Are dictators trying to achieve a similar goal?

# CHAPTER THREE

# Living in a dictatorship

We have learnt how dictators take power and do everything possible to hold on to it. However, what do we know about the people who live under a dictatorship? Around one-third of the world's population, including more than 1 billion people in China, live in countries in which they are unable to choose their leaders. What is life like for them and how does it compare to life in a democracy?

## ALWAYS BAD?

It would be a mistake to think that dictatorships are always bad for all their people. Although his harsh regime grew to be hated and ended in violence, Muammar Gaddafi's dictatorship in Libya used some of the money it made from selling oil to improve education and living conditions for many of the country's people. Dictators may sometimes bring peace and stability to a country that is torn apart by civil war. Dictatorships may also provide stability in a country in which there are a number of violent political groups that could bring about war and bloodshed if they were allowed to attempt to gain control.

*Forms of government other than dictatorships exist in which people's rights are restricted. Saudi Arabia is a monarchy in which ordinary people have little say in government.*

A group of friends meeting at a restaurant or communicating online would be seen as suspicious in many of the world's dictatorships.

## PAYING THE PRICE

There is often a high price to pay for the stability gained through dictatorship. People in a dictatorship lose many of the rights that are enjoyed by those who live in a democracy. In some dictatorships, people live in constant fear of being arrested or imprisoned without any protection from the law. In the cruellest of dictatorships, millions of people may even lose their lives because of the wishes or prejudices of a dictator. People often count the price of dictatorship for many years after a dictator is no longer in power.

## UNDERSTANDING BETTER

### LOSING HUMAN RIGHTS

To understand the experience of living under a dictatorship, consider the things you enjoy in a democracy that you would lose in a dictatorship:

- The right to vote at elections.

- The right to speak and write whatever you please.

- The right to hold whatever political or religious beliefs you choose.

- Protection from independent police and law courts.

Do you think these rights are worth having? Which is the most important to you and why?

# Living in fear

In 1989, many of the communist dictatorships that once held power in Eastern Europe collapsed. The citizens of East Germany discovered that the Stasi secret police had kept a detailed file for every citizen. These files now occupy more than 100 kilometres (62 miles) of shelf space. Those who lived through the East German dictatorship can now see their files and how the government was watching every aspect of their lives.

### UNDER WATCH

People living in dictatorships are used to being watched. Security cameras watch the streets. Their neighbours, or even other family members, may be forced to spy on them. Any small sign of opposition to the dictatorship, even a few careless words, could mean a person loses a job or is **interrogated** or imprisoned without trial.

### THE LAW OF DICTATORSHIP

In the most extreme dictatorships, thousands of people may be murdered simply for disagreeing with the dictatorship. Suspects can be tortured to gain information. In a country in which the only law is that of the dictator, ordinary people have no protection and live in constant fear for their lives.

*Modern dictatorships use the latest technology to keep watch over people.*

# UNDERSTANDING BETTER

## THE SCARS OF DICTATORSHIP

"The stories are always in the back of my head whether I'm lying in bed or out in social situations. I find it hard to trust people."

A former East German citizen explains the impact that constant spying by security forces has had on her life. Can you think of other ways in which people's lives might be affected long after they stop living in a dictatorship?

*These protestors are carrying pictures of people who were tried or imprisoned unfairly during Franco's dictatorship in Spain.*

### FIGHTING FEAR

While people living under a dictatorship have little chance to protest, international human rights organizations, such as Human Rights Watch and Amnesty International, will often campaign for the release of political prisoners. These organizations are constantly raising awareness of the plight of people who are wrongly imprisoned under extreme dictatorships.

# Finding scapegoats

Life can often be especially difficult for particular groups of a population living under a dictatorship. We have seen that one method dictators use to unite their people is to find a convenient enemy, often within their country. Saddam Hussein persecuted the Kurdish minority living in the north of Iraq and even used chemical weapons against them. Probably the most catastrophic example of this type of persecution was Hitler's treatment of the Jews.

### THE HOLOCAUST

Hitler attacked the Jews in his early speeches as he sought to gain control of Germany. After the dictator came to power in 1933, he began to persecute Jewish businesses. Jews were stripped of their rights as German citizens. Other groups Hitler attacked included **Roma** people and homosexuals.

During World War II, Hitler and his supporters began to murder vast numbers of Jews. It is believed that 6 million of the 9.5 million Jews who had lived in Europe before World War II were killed during Hitler's regime. This mass murder of the Jews is known as the **Holocaust**.

*These photographs show some of the millions of victims of Hitler's Holocaust.*

## COULD IT HAPPEN AGAIN?

The Holocaust is one of the most horrific crimes in history, yet similar atrocities are still happening around the world. Omar al-Bashir, the dictator of Sudan, originally came to power as military dictator and has since been elected by the Sudanese. The dictator is wanted by the International Criminal Court for war crimes, including allowing the murder of thousands of civilians in the Darfur region of Sudan.

# UNDERSTANDING BETTER

## HOW DID IT HAPPEN?

The information you have discovered about dictatorships should help you to understand how something as terrible as the Holocaust could happen. The Jews were a distinct group in German society. This helped Hitler to single them out and blame them for Germany's problems. Other factors that lead to the persecution of a group of people within a dictatorship include:

- The dictatorship's control of the media.

- People's fear of opposing a brutal regime that could easily arrest and imprison them.

- The cult of personality built around a dictator such as Adolf Hitler.

All these things help to explain why ordinary people did not prevent the terrible crimes against the Jews from taking place in Nazi Germany.

*This is the gate to the Auschwitz **concentration camp** in which poison gas was used to murder thousands of people. The site is preserved to remind people of the horrors of the Holocaust in Nazi Germany.*

# CHAPTER FOUR

# Fighting against dictatorship

It can be extremely difficult for people to fight back against a dictatorship because ordinary people within an **oppressive** regime have so little power. Thankfully, all of history's dictatorships have eventually come to an end. Some of them ended in violence, others ended when the dictator allowed a gradual transition towards democracy.

### WHY DO DICTATORSHIPS DIE?

Sometimes, the answer to this question is obvious. Dictators may spend a lot of time and effort convincing people that they are all-powerful, but eventually all dictators grow old and die. Often, the dictator's government dies with them.

### LONG-LASTING DICTATORSHIPS

Some dictatorships are able to endure because in these regimes power is not held by one single person. The current government of China is such a dictatorship – the people cannot vote against it and criticism of the government is not usually allowed. The Chinese government has held power since 1949 because, since the death of its founder Mao Zedong, the government has not depended on the power and personality of one single leader.

In 2012, Myanmar's military dictatorship introduced limited democracy. Finally, democracy campaigner Aung San Suu Kyi (seen second from right) was elected to parliament after years of house arrest.

The statues of Saddam Hussein that once stood in Iraqi cities are now in pieces, torn apart by the country's people when they were liberated from the dictator's horrific regime.

## THE INTERNATIONAL COMMUNITY

The United Nations is an organization made up of nearly all the countries on Earth. Its goals include promoting peace and security around the world and protecting human rights. The organization's powers include the right to impose **sanctions** to stop other countries trading with dictators. In extreme cases, the United Nations may also allow countries to take military action against a dictatorship. This happened in 1991 when international troops forced Saddam Hussein's Iraqi army to end its invasion of Kuwait.

## UNDERSTANDING BETTER

### WHY DO DICTATORS NOT GIVE UP?

Saddam Hussein was able to stay in power in Iraq for more than 30 years by combining a brutal regime with a series of wars against his country's neighbours. The dictator was swept from power by a coalition of forces in 2003. Why did Saddam choose to defy the international community in a way that led to his downfall? Maybe he started to believe in his own cult of personality. What do you think?

# Defeating dictators

Dictators survive by building a state apparatus that supports them and prevents others from challenging them. They restrict access to the media, so different points of view cannot be expressed. Dictatorships imprison those who disagree with them. However, well-organized opposition can often triumph against dictators. How is this achieved?

Cambodia in Southeast Asia suffered many decades of war and dictatorship. It has now achieved some political stability, showing that even the most brutal dictatorships can be overcome.

## PEOPLE POWER

One reason why dictatorships spend so much time showing how strong they are is because they know that their power may be based on shaky foundations. A dictator may have only a very small group of supporters, especially when compared to the population of a country as a whole. In 1989, the people of Romania demonstrated against their dictator, Nicolae Ceausescu. The dictator used his army to attack the protestors, but the demonstrations just became bigger and bigger, until Ceausescu was eventually forced from power.

## TRIGGERING PROTESTS

Protests that overthrow a dictatorship can be triggered by a number of situations. Sometimes they are a response to changes in another country. This was the case when waves of protests swept the Arab world in 2011 – the protests in one Arabic country ignited protests in other Arabic countries. Sometimes the government can trigger rebellion, for example, by arresting an opponent and infuriating the country's people so much that they rise up against the regime. Sometimes, the trigger for revolution might be a general problem such as high food prices.

## MILITARY REVOLT

Dictators always depend on the loyalty of the armed forces, which are likely to be more heavily armed than ordinary citizens. Military personnel are trained to follow orders, but they also endure life under a harsh dictatorship. When a large part of the armed forces decides to switch sides and supports the opposition, as happened in Libya in 2011, a dictatorship cannot survive.

*The Berlin Wall once divided the city of Berlin and was a symbol of East Germany's dictatorship. This section of wall includes a picture of deposed Libyan dictator Muammar Gaddafi.*

# The Arab Spring

In December 2010, a protest by street seller Mohamed Bouazizi in Tunisia triggered a series of rebellions against dictatorships, which swept across North Africa and the Arab world the following year. Some rebellions succeeded, some were ended by brutal force and others still continue. This wave of protest was called the "Arab Spring".

## DICTATORS DISMISSED

A few weeks after the Arab protests began, the governments of Tunisia and Egypt were toppled. President Mubarak of Egypt was forced from power when his army refused to open fire on huge demonstrations in the capital city, Cairo.

## DICTATORS HOLD ON

Elsewhere in the Arab world, dictators were not dismissed so easily. In Yemen, months of protests forced President Ali Abdullah Saleh to hand over power to his deputy. Since then, Yemen has been torn by war and terrorism. In Bahrain, the protests were brutally suppressed, with help from troops of neighbouring country Saudi Arabia.

▼ *Young people were often at the centre of protests during the Arab Spring.*

## WHICH DICTATORSHIPS WILL SURVIVE?

In 2011, the Arab Spring was seen as a great wave of freedom sweeping the region. However, the transfer to democracy is not always easy. In Egypt, there were fears that the people had exchanged one dictatorship for another through the rebellion when the military took power and a new president granted himself extra powers. Fighting between different factions in Libya has continued long after the death of Gaddafi. Discover the latest news about these uprisings and ask yourself which do you think will succeed in the long term and why?

*Foreign newspapers report the death of Gaddafi, who had supported terrorism abroad as well as oppressing his own people.*

### FIGHTING FOR THEIR LIVES

In Libya, rebel forces battled against Muammar Gaddafi for many months, with some military help from the international community. Eventually the dictator was caught and killed, but not without huge damage and lasting divisions in Libya. Bashar al-Assad, the dictator of Syria, refused to leave power, unleashing death, destruction and civil war on the people he claimed to lead. Syria is still under the dictator's iron grip.

# CHAPTER FIVE

# A future for dictatorships?

The early successes of the Arab Spring suggested that dictatorships were in retreat in many parts of the world as people embraced democracy. Dictators face many forces that make it difficult for them to hold on to power, but there are still many dictatorships in place around the world.

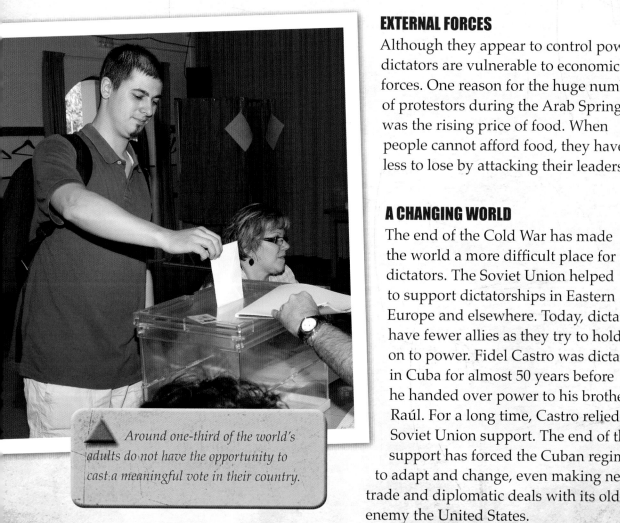

Around one-third of the world's adults do not have the opportunity to cast a meaningful vote in their country.

## EXTERNAL FORCES

Although they appear to control power, dictators are vulnerable to economic forces. One reason for the huge numbers of protestors during the Arab Spring was the rising price of food. When people cannot afford food, they have less to lose by attacking their leaders.

## A CHANGING WORLD

The end of the Cold War has made the world a more difficult place for dictators. The Soviet Union helped to support dictatorships in Eastern Europe and elsewhere. Today, dictators have fewer allies as they try to hold on to power. Fidel Castro was dictator in Cuba for almost 50 years before he handed over power to his brother, Raúl. For a long time, Castro relied on Soviet Union support. The end of that support has forced the Cuban regime to adapt and change, even making new trade and diplomatic deals with its old enemy the United States.

## STILL IN CHARGE

Despite significant global changes, there are still dictators in many countries around the world. Also in power are leaders who claim to be democratic but run unfair elections to make sure they are never voted out. New dictatorships are also taking control of some areas of the world where uncertainity and upheaval make it easy for dictators to move in.

## UNDERSTANDING BETTER

### DICTATORS.COM

Use of the internet has grown dramatically since 2000. Today, around 40 per cent of the world's people are online. Do you think this is likely to help dictators or make life more difficult for them? Online communication can cross national boundaries, but it can also spread ideas very quickly. Could dictators use the internet to spread their own ideas? Rather than crushing internet use, will dictators of the future found their regimes on this form of communication? What do you think?

*Vladimir Putin has been president or prime minister of Russia since 1999, and he is undoubtedly a popular leader. However, international observers have questioned whether Russian elections are fair and if critics of the Putin regime have been harshly treated.*

# A family of dictators

No one knew much about North Korea's new leader Kim Jong-un when he took power in 2011. Information about his life had been kept secret. The public did know that he was the youngest son of Kim Jong-il, who held power for 17 years and had succeeded his own father, Kim Il-sung. In 1948, Kim Il-sung established North Korea's communist government, called the Democratic People's Republic of Korea (DPRK). For nearly 70 years since then, the members of the Kim family have been the dictators of North Korea.

## TIGHT CONTROL

Since gaining power, the Kims have imposed a strict regime in the country. Information is tightly controlled – both coming into and out of the country. Mobile phones can be used but not to call other countries. The media is censored, too. The internet is very different in North Korea. Only a few thousand people have real access to the internet, mostly poltical leaders, their families and some carefully chosen students.

## SPEAKING OUT

People who speak out against the government can be sent to gulags. These are harsh labour and prison camps where many die from bad working conditions and malnutrition.

*This North Korean stamp was issued in 1969 and shows Kim Il-sung, who controlled North Korea from 1948 to 1994.*

위대한 수령 김일성동지는 영원히 우리와 함께 계신다

A poster in North Korea depicts Kim Il-sung and states "Great leader with us" in Korean.

### MAKING THREATS

Outsiders have wondered whether Kim Jong-un will be different from his father and grandfather. Maybe a younger man would relax the country's tough regime? Perhaps he would introduce a more modern approach to politics within his country? It seems that these hopes may not be fulfilled. Instead, since 2013, Kim Jong-un's government has issued a series of threats against its neighbour South Korea – and even against the United States. The world waits to see what will happen in this extremely secretive dictatorship.

## UNDERSTANDING BETTER

### ANALYSE PROPAGANDA

North Korea uses propaganda to present positive images of its leaders. Propaganda is the spreading of information or ideas to promote a certain cause. The information may not be realistic and may even be false.

After reading about life in North Korea, examine the image on this page. It shows a poster in North Korea portraying the former leader Kim Il-sung. What information is the poster trying to convey? Do you think this information is true or misleading? Does it help you to understand the text better?

# What have you learnt?

Throughout this book, we have learnt that dictatorships take many forms. We know that they have existed since ancient times, with the Roman general Julius Caesar becoming one of the first Roman dictators. Most of the world's dictators have ruled since 1900, using mass communication and military strength to support their governments. Some dictators, such as Adolf Hitler and Joseph Stalin, are responsible for mass murder on a horrifying scale.

## UNDERSTANDING DICTATORSHIPS

We have discovered how dictators gain and keep power. We know how they manipulate the media and use propaganda to convince people that dictatorship is best for them. We have also learnt that, as the Romans knew, strong leadership can be a good thing in times of crisis. However, too often dictators are focused only on keeping their own power, while ignoring the rights and wishes of the people they lead. We have discovered how people can fight back against dictators, even if they have no political voice.

*The United Kingdom has often fought against dictators. Recent examples include Saddam Hussein in Iraq and the Taliban dictatorship that ruled Afghanistan.*

*Many people in China have become wealthy in recent years, but most of these people have very little political power.*

## AN END TO DICTATORSHIP?

Recent years have seen the end of many long-serving dictators, such as Muammar Gaddafi and Saddam Hussein. Others, such as the military dictatorship in Myanmar, have achieved a move towards greater democracy. However, dictatorships in some countries remain extremely strong – and the end of dictatorship in these parts of the world still seems a long way off.

# UNDERSTANDING BETTER

## WHAT NOW?

Using what you have learnt about dictators, study some of the dictatorships around the world to find out how they operate. How do these dictatorships treat their people and what would happen if they were no longer there? How do countries living under a dictatorship differ from your own?

# GLOSSARY

**absolute power** government in which no challenge to authority is allowed

**ally** country that stands together with others in a fight against something

**citizen** member of a country

**civil war** internal conflict between two, or more, groups in a country

**colony** country that is ruled over by another country, as part of an empire

**communist** system of government where the state controls all wealth and property

**concentration camp** prison camp where large groups of people are imprisoned, usually without having been convicted of a crime

**congress** group of people who are elected to help to govern the United States

**constitution** set of rules and principles that lays down how a nation should be governed

**consul** senior elected officer of a government, first used in the ancient Roman republic

**democracy** system in which the government is voted for by most or all of the adults in that country

**deposing** forcing to leave power

**dictatorship** government by a leader who rules with absolute power

**emperor** someone who rules over an empire

**exiling** forcing a person to leave a country

**Holocaust** organized murder of millions of Jews, and other groups, before and during World War II

**human right** right that every human being has, regardless of where they live

**informant** person who passes information about other people to the police or other authority

**institution** organization that has particular systems

**interrogated** questioned harshly

**media** means of communication that can reach large numbers of people, such as radio or television broadcasts

**monarch** king or queen who rules in a monarchy

**oppressive** controlling with force

**persecuted** treated harshly, or singled out for harsh treatment

**political party** group of people with similar ideas about how a country should be run

**propaganda** information spread in order to influence public opinion or present the person creating the information in a favourable way

**regime** type of government that strictly controls a country

**rigging** using dishonest ways to control the result of something, such as an election

**Roma** group of travelling people who originally came from Asia but are now found across the world

**sanction** law that prevents a country from buying goods from, or selling them to, other countries

**secret police** security officers who maintain security within a country with a secretive or repressive government

**Soviet Union** union of countries in Eastern Europe, led by Russia, which lasted until 1991

**suppressed** kept down

**suspected** believed to be guilty of doing something wrong

**tyrant** cruel and oppressive ruler

**United Nations** organization that includes representatives of most countries in the world, and that rules in cases of international disputes

# FIND OUT MORE

## BOOKS

*Ancient Greece* (Hardnuts of History), Tracey Turner (A&C Black, 2014)

*Dastardly Dictators, Rulers and other Loony Leaders* (Barmy Biogs), Paul Harrison (Wayland, 2013)

*Julius Caesar and the Romans* (History Starting Points), David Gill (Franklin Watts, 2016)

*Napoleon Bonaparte* (Extaordinary Lives), Juith Henegan (Wayland, 2010)

*Political Messages and Propaganda* (Getting the Message), Sean Connolly (Franklin Watts, 2009)

*Propaganda* (World War II Sourcebook), Charlie Samuels (Wayland, 2013)

*Uprisings in the Middle East* (Behind the News), Philip Steele (Wayland, 2014)

## WEBSITES

Visit the BBC News website to discover the story of the Arab Spring in countries across North Africa and the Middle East:
**www.bbc.co.uk/news/world-middle-east-12813859**

Discover who were the worst Roman dictators, at:
**www.historyextra.com/article/international-history/8-bloodiest-roman-emperors-history**

Explore dictatorship in Nazi Germany, at:
**www.historylearningsite.co.uk/nazi-germany/nazi-germany-dictatorship/**

Follow the life and dictatorship of Saddam Hussein, at:
**news.bbc.co.uk/1/shared/spl/hi/middle_east/03/v3_iraq_timeline/html**

Read more about how dictatorship works, at:
**people.howstuffworks.com/dictator.htm**

# INDEX